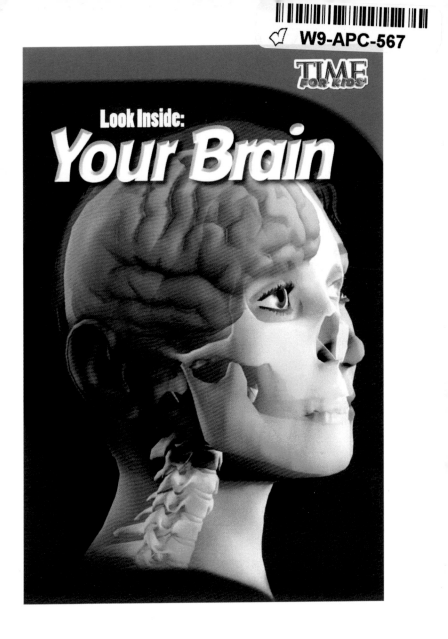

TIME
FOR KIDS

Look Inside:
Your Brain

Ben Williams

Consultant

Timothy Rasinski, Ph.D.
Kent State University

Publishing Credits

Dona Herweck Rice, *Editor-in-Chief*

Robin Erickson, *Production Director*

Lee Aucoin, *Creative Director*

Conni Medina, M.A.Ed., *Editorial Director*

Jamey Acosta, *Editor*

Stephanie Reid, *Photo Editor*

Rachelle Cracchiolo, M.S.Ed., *Publisher*

Image Credits

Cover Illustration by Rick Nease p.4 Toria/Shutterstock; p.5 Monkey Business Images/
Shutterstock; p.6 sextoacto/Shutterstock; p.6 sextoacto/Shutterstock; p.7 pixdeluxe/
iStockphoto; p.8 geniuscook_com/Shutterstock; p.9 top: jetsetmodels/Shutterstock; p.9
botttom: Photosani/Shutterstock; p.10 top: marilyn barbone/Shutterstock; p.10 bottom:
Craig Craver/Photolibrary; p.11 left: JBryson/iStockphoto; p.11 right: Tomasz Markowski/
Shutterstock; p.12 bjones27/iStockphoto; p.12 bjones27/iStockphoto; p.13 ktaylorg/
iStockphoto; p.14 Steve Cole/iStockphoto; p.15 AVAVA/Shutterstock; p.16 Sebastian
Kaulitzki/Shutterstock; p.17 Rick Nease; p.18 top: interactimages/Shutterstock; p.18 bottom:
THEGIFT777/iStockphoto; p.19 top: pflorendo/iStockphoto; p.19 left: interactimages/
Shutterstock; p.19 right: Paczyuk Svitlana/Shutterstock; p.22-23 Sebastian Kaulitzki/
Shutterstock; p.24 sjlocke/iStockphoto; p.25 top: bowdenimages/iStockphoto; p.25 bottom:
Jane September/Shutterstock; p.26 top: Zurijeta/Shutterstock; p.26 bottom: bonniej/
iStockphoto; p.27 MichaelDeLeon/iStockphoto; p.28 martan/Shutterstock;
tback cover Photosani/Shutterstock

Based on writing from *TIME For Kids*.

TIME For Kids and the *TIME For Kids* logo are registered trademarks of TIME Inc.
Used under license.

Teacher Created Materials

5301 Oceanus Drive
Huntington Beach, CA 92649-1030
http://www.tcmpub.com
ISBN 978-1-4333-3634-8
© 2012 Teacher Created Materials, Inc.
Reprinted 2013

Table of Contents

The World's Fastest Computer 4

What Is a Brain? 8

How the Brain Works 16

Parts of the Brain 22

Use Your Noodle 24

A Healthy Brain 26

Glossary 28

The World's Fastest Computer

There is an amazing computer. It is faster than any other computer in the world. It can understand speech and writing. It can come up with new ideas. It can make plans. It can control a whole, complicated system and do many things at once without shutting down.

In fact, the more it is used, the better it gets.

What is this amazing computer? It is your brain, of course!

Superbrain!

How fast is your brain? Some people say that it can handle 10 quadrillion instructions each second. That's 10,000,000,000,000,000!

What Is a Brain?

Most animals have a brain. But your brain—the human brain—is the most amazing brain of all. It is larger and more complicated than most brains.

The human brain sits inside the **skull** at the top and back of the head. It is about the size of a small cauliflower, and it is shaped a little like one, too.

The brain is very important. That is why it is protected by the hard skull bones.

Animal Brains

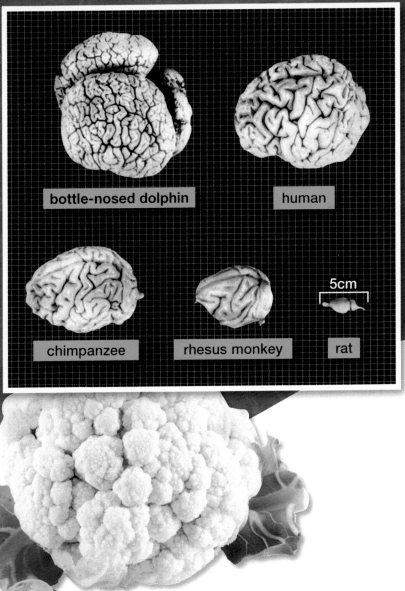

bottle-nosed dolphin

human

chimpanzee

rhesus monkey

5cm

rat

Touch your finger to your nose. Clap
your hands. Sing a song. You can do all
of these things because your brain tells
your body what to do.

Your brain is always on the job. It is like a boss and all the parts of your body are the workers. All you have to do is think a thought and your brain makes the workers get right to it.

For example, if you want to run, your brain thinks, "Run," and your legs and feet do their jobs.

If you want to eat, your brain sends a message to all the right parts. Just like that, you are eating.

Your brain is so amazing that it can make your body do some things without you needing to think about them. You breathe without thinking. Your heart beats without thinking. Your body temperature stays just right. These are just some of the things your brain handles on its own.

Who Is in Charge?

You can think about breathing, but you do not have to tell your brain to do it. Your brain will keep you breathing whether you think about it or not.

How the Brain Works

The brain is part of the **nervous system**. It works with the **spinal cord** and the **nerves**. They work together to control and balance the body, mind, and emotions.

Neuron Activity

Neurons send messages to the body to tell it what to do. The bright orange lights in the picture are the neuron messages.

neuron cell

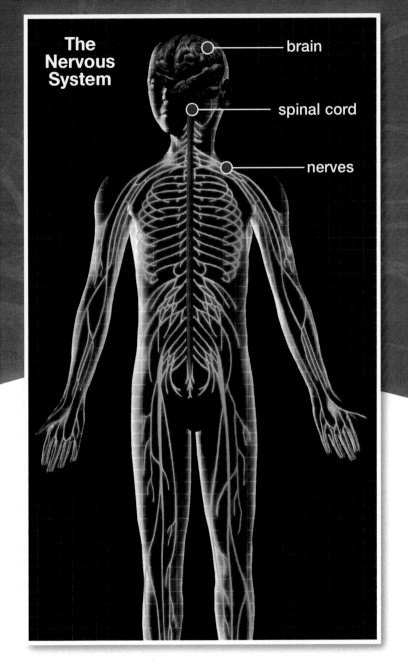

The Nervous System

brain

spinal cord

nerves

The brain takes in information from outside the body. Then it sends the information through the body using the nervous system.

To get information, the brain uses the five senses: sight, hearing, touch, smell, and taste.

When you use your senses, you are using your brain.

To send information, the brain uses **neurons** (NOOR-onz). Neurons are nerve cells. They can be found throughout the body. They send messages to each other.

Each neuron is made of three main parts: **cell body**, **axon**, and **nerve ending**.

Neurons

Neurons come in many sizes. The axon of a single neuron can run from your fingertip through your whole arm. But neurons in the brain can be shorter than your shortest eyelash.

nerve ending

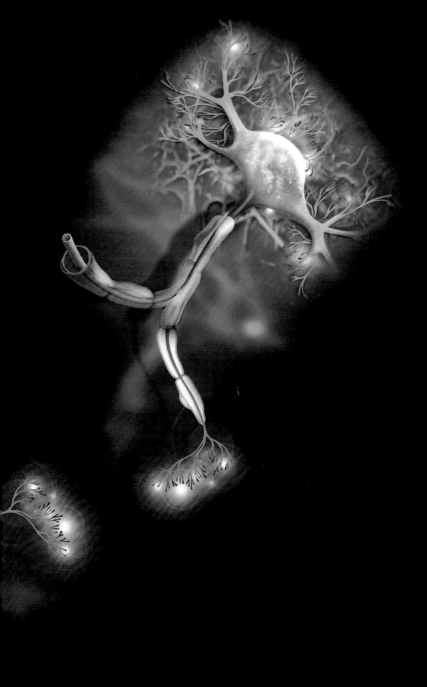

Parts of the Brain

The brain is made of the **brainstem**, the **cerebellum** (ser-uh-BEL-uhm), and the **forebrain**.

The brainstem is in charge of the things we do without thinking, like breathing. It is also in charge of moving our arms and legs, digesting food, and getting rid of waste.

The cerebellum makes the parts of our body work together so that we stay balanced.

The forebrain controls our body temperature and our emotions. It puts together the information it gets from the senses. It holds our memories for us, and it lets us think.

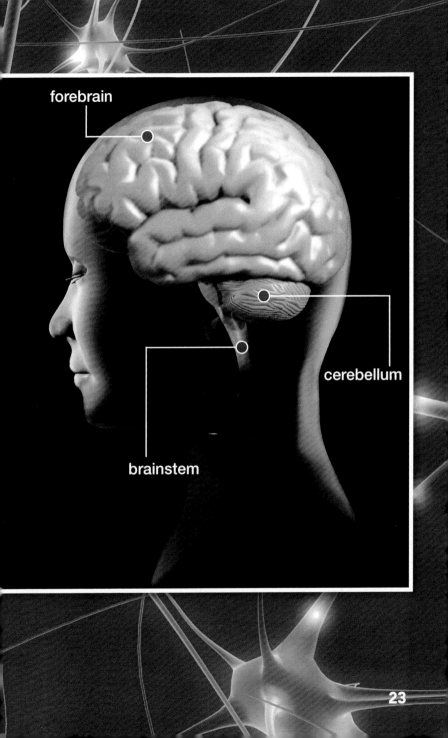

forebrain

cerebellum

brainstem

23

Use Your Noodle

Has anyone ever told you to use your noodle? Have they said to put on your thinking cap? These are just two of the funny names people use for the brain. They tell us to keep thinking.

It is important to use your brain when you want to do something. The brain will tell you how to do it. It will tell

you if it is right or wrong, and it will tell you if it is safe.

If you are not sure about something, just use your noodle! It will help you figure it out.

A Healthy Brain

How can you keep your brain healthy? Everything in your body works best with good food and lots of water. Exercise is important, too.

How can you exercise your brain? Use it! Use it at school and at play. Think new thoughts and try new games.

Your brain likes to be used. So, use your brain and keep it strong!

Glossary

axon—the part of the neuron that sends impulses away from the cell body

brainstem—the area at the base of the brain that is in charge of things we do without thinking

cell body—the area of a nerve cell that has a nucleus and cytoplasm

cerebellum—a large portion of the back of the brain that is concerned with bodily balance

forebrain—the forwardmost part of the brain that controls body temperature and emotions

nerve ending—the place where the nerve ends

nerves—the little sensors throughout the body that send and receive messages

nervous system—the system in the body (made of the brain, spinal cord, and nerves) that allows the body to think, remember, feel, and do things

neurons—the impulse-conducting cells

skull—the bones inside the head that form together and protect the brain

spinal cord—the long, thin cord made of nerve tissue that extends from the brain